Then We'll Say Goodnight

Written by
Marianne Hesse

Illustrated by
Angela Paul

LUMINARE PRESS
WWW.LUMINAREPRESS.COM

Then We'll Say Goodnight
Copyright © 2020 by Marianne Hesse

All rights reserved. This book or any portion thereof may not be reproduced or used in any manner whatsoever without the express written permission of the publisher, except for the use of brief quotations in a book review.

Printed in the United States of America

Illustrations by Angela Paul
Production design by Claire Flint Last

Luminare Press
442 Charnelton St.
Eugene, OR 97401
www.luminarepress.com

LCCN: 2020920905
ISBN: 978-1-64388-540-7

*For Denny Plesea, the best friend a dog could ever have
and for Micah and his inquisitive Mr. Bun.
—Marianne Hesse*

*To my loving parents, Luise and Marcus,
who have always supported me and my art.
—Angela Paul*

Puppers, puppers, everywhere
In my bed and in my hair

Puppers, puppers, go away
Now is not the time to play

Puppers, puppers, can't you see
You have got to let me be

Puppers, puppers, if you do
When I get up, I'll play with you

Puppers, puppers, settle down
Careful or you'll tear my gown

Puppers, why are you so bad?
If you don't stop, you'll make me mad

Puppers, I am warning you
I mean it now, I really do

Puppers, puppers, now you did it
You're going to your own bed right this minute!

One kiss,
   then we'll say goodnight.

About the Author
Marianne Hesse

Despite a surfeit of life experience, the author has continued to have limited success in getting her own errant puppies back to bed. She lives in San Francisco, and *Then We'll Say Goodnight* is her first children's book.